Science Enquiry

HOW ARE ANIMALS GROUPED?

Lisa M. Bolt Simons

Raintree is an imprint of Capstone Global Library Limited, a company incorporated in England and Wales having its registered office at 264 Banbury Road, Oxford, OX2 7DY – Registered company number: 6695582

www.raintree.co.uk
myorders@raintree.co.uk

Edited by Erika L. Shores
Designed by Dina Her and Juliette Peters
Original illustrations © Capstone Global Library Limited 2022
Picture research by Eric Gohl and Kelly Garvin
Production by Tori Abraham
Originated by Capstone Global Library Ltd
Printed and bound in India

978 1 3982 2526 8 (hardback)
978 1 3982 2525 1 (paperback)

British Library Cataloguing in Publication Data
A full catalogue record for this book is available from the British Library.

Acknowledgements
We would like to thank the following for permission to reproduce photographs: iStockphoto/Eraxion, 25; Shutterstock: aaltair, 7 (sea star), Alexey Seafarer, 7 (polar bear), Andrey Pavlov, 7 (ant), Andrey Snider-Bell, 27, AnujinM, 7 (deer), Beatrice Prezzemoli, 14, bebek_moto, 16, bogdan ionescu, 7 (salamander), Butterfly Hunter, 7 (butterfly), cwieders, 13, Damsea, 29, Darryl Vest, 22, Dirk Ercken, 15, DWI YULIANTO, cover (bottom left), Elnur, 11, Eric Isselee, 7 (frog, peacock, snake), F.Rubion, 17, fivespots, 7 (turtle), FloridaStock, 7 (eagle), Harry Collins Photography, 20, JaySi, 10, Kerimili, 1, 28, Kongkham35Gmail.com, 5, Konstantin Novikov, 24, LeonP, 7 (shark), Levent Konuk, 7 (clown fish), Mrinal Pal, cover (bottom right), pets in frames, 7 (tarantula), Ralph Eshelman, 21, Rostislav Stefanek, 18, TheLazyPineapple, cover (middle left), thka, 9 (top), Veronika 7833, 9 (bottom), Victor Shova, cover (top), Villiers Steyn, 12, wildestanimal, 19, worldwildlifewonders, 23, yanikap, 26.
Artistic elements: Shutterstock/balabolka.

CONTENTS

INVESTIGATION: HOW DO WE GROUP? 4

WHY DO SCIENTISTS GROUP ANIMALS? 8

HOW DO SCIENTISTS GROUP ANIMALS? 12

WHICH ANIMALS ARE VERTEBRATES? 14

WHICH ANIMALS ARE INVERTEBRATES? 24

GLOSSARY 30

FIND OUT MORE 31

INDEX 32

Words in **bold** are in the glossary.

INVESTIGATION: HOW DO WE GROUP?

Your clean clothes are mixed up in a basket. Look at the characteristics or features. What is the same? What is different? Put clothes with the same characteristics in the same place. Then they are easier to find. Shirts in one drawer. Socks in another. Dresses and skirts in the wardrobe. You just grouped the clothes!

The same thing happens at zoos. Zookeepers understand the characteristics of different animals. Then they build **habitats**. The animals get grouped!

Now let's do a grouping activity.
Look at the animals on page 7.
Make **observations**. Think about
the characteristics or features.
In science these are called **traits**. Do
the animals have legs? Do they have
feathers? Do they have fur?

Think about what is the same.
Think about what is different.
How would you group these animals?

Take a piece of paper. Write
the animal names. Then group the
animals. List traits that are the same.

ant

butterfly

clownfish

deer

eagle

frog

peacock

polar bear

salamander

sea star

shark

snake

spider

turtle

WHY DO SCIENTISTS GROUP ANIMALS?

Scientists can name and describe more than 1 million **species** of animals. That's a lot of animals!

Animals are part of our daily lives. Some animals are pets. Some animals live in our gardens. Some animals **pollinate** plants. These animals help humans. Other animals such as ticks are **parasites**. They can cause humans problems. With so many animals in the world, why do scientists group them?

Remember how sorted animals help people find them in a zoo? Fish live with fish. Otters live with otters. Bats live with bats. Imagine if zookeepers had 1 million animals in a zoo!

Scientists put animals into groups so that it is easier to learn about them. Scientists can keep track of all the ways animals are alike and different.

HOW DO SCIENTISTS GROUP ANIMALS?

All animals are put into two main groups. Animals with backbones, or spines, make up one group. They are **vertebrates**. Animals without backbones make up the second group. They are **invertebrates**.

Vertebrates are sorted into classes. The biggest classes are amphibians, reptiles, birds, fish and mammals.

A lion is a vertebrate.

Invertebrates are sorted into many groups called **phyla**. The phylum with the most invertebrates are **arthropods**.

Think about your investigation. Did you group vertebrates and invertebrates?

A spider is an invertebrate.

WHICH ANIMALS ARE VERTEBRATES?

Have you ever seen a frog jump by a pond? Frogs are amphibians. Salamanders are too. Amphibians are cold-blooded. Their body temperature changes with the temperature of their surroundings. They breathe through their moist skin. They lay eggs. They live on land and in the water.

salamander

poison dart frog

Amphibians can be almost any colour! Some really stand out, though. They are bright blue, green and red. They can be poisonous. The poison dart frog is the most poisonous animal in the world.

python

Snakes are reptiles without legs. Other reptiles, such as alligators and lizards, have legs. Turtles have legs and a shell.

Reptiles are cold-blooded like amphibians. But their skin is covered with scales or plates. They breathe with lungs. Most reptiles lay eggs. Some live on land. Others live in water.

The longest reptiles are python snakes and saltwater crocodiles. They can grow more than 6 metres (20 feet) long!

saltwater crocodile

Think about a fish in a lake. A fish is a swimming vertebrate. Fish have **gills** to breathe. They have scales and fins. They are cold-blooded like reptiles and amphibians.

Some fish live in freshwater. Trout and carp live in lakes and rivers. Other fish live in saltwater. Clownfish and snappers live in the sea.

trout

shark

Sharks and stingrays are also fish. But they don't have a full bony skeleton. Sharks and stingrays are in a small class of vertebrates. They have skeletons of **cartilage**.

falcon

Look up in the sky. See a bird? It's a flying vertebrate! All birds have feathers and wings. But not all birds fly. Ostriches can't fly. But they run fast. Penguins don't fly. But they swim fast.

All birds have beaks or bills. Birds also lay eggs. Birds are warm-blooded. Warm-blooded animals keep the inside of their bodies the same temperature all the time.

A penguin with egg and chick

The last group of vertebrates are mammals. Look in the mirror. You're a mammal! Mammals have hair or fur. Like birds, they are warm-blooded. Most mammals have live babies. The babies drink the mother's milk.

Mammals breathe air. Mammals that live in water still need air. Whales and dolphins live in the water but come up to breathe.

dolphins

platypus

Sometimes mammals look like other vertebrates. A bat is a flying mammal. A platypus is a mammal that looks like a duck. It even lays eggs!

WHICH ANIMALS ARE INVERTEBRATES?

Scientists also group animals without backbones. They are called invertebrates. They are the largest group of animals. Imagine a pie chart made of animals. Almost all of the pie chart would be invertebrates!

squid

mite

You need a microscope to see the smallest invertebrate. It is called a mite. The biggest invertebrate has eyes the size of basketballs! It is a giant squid.

dragonfly

Sit outside. The largest group of invertebrates will keep you company. They are arthropods.

Insects are the largest group of arthropods. They have six legs. There are flying ones such as butterflies and dragonflies. There are biting ones such as mosquitoes. There are working ones like bees.

Other arthropods have more than six legs. Spiders and scorpions have eight legs. Crabs and lobsters have 10 legs. Millipedes have as many as 750 legs!

scorpion

Like vertebrates, invertebrates are grouped based on their traits. They are also grouped on their bodies and life cycles. Invertebrates include ocean animals like jellyfish and coral. Snails, clams and octopi are grouped together. Starfish and sea urchins are in another group.

jellyfish

starfish

There are so many animals in the world. It is easier for scientists to name and teach us about grouped animals. Scientists can also study and understand them better in groups.

Look back at your investigation. Would you change any of your groupings? Keep investigating!

GLOSSARY

arthropod invertebrate with a segmented body and jointed legs

cartilage bendy, flexible tissue in animals

gill organ on a fish to breathe

habitat place where a plant or animal lives

invertebrate animal without a backbone

observation something that you have noticed by watching carefully

phyla plural of phylum, a class of organisms

pollinate take pollen from a flower to another flower

species group of animals or plants with common characteristics or features

trait characteristic or feature

vertebrate animal with a backbone

FIND OUT MORE

BOOKS

Animal Groups series, Amy Kortuem, Lucia Raatma and Martha E. H. Rustad (Raintree, 2020)

Knowledge Encyclopedia: Animal!, John Woodward (DK Children, 2016)

Mammals (Animal Kingdom), Lisa J. Amstutz (Raintree, 2018)

WEBSITES

kids.nationalgeographic.com/animals
Read more about the different types of animal with National Geographic.

www.bbc.co.uk/bitesize/topics/zn22pv4/articles/z3nbcwx
Learn more about animal classification with BBC Bitesize.

www.dkfindout.com/uk/animals-and-nature/animal-kingdom/classifying-animals/
DKFindout! shows you how animals are classified.

INDEX

amphibians 12, 14, 15, 16, 18
arthropods 13, 26, 27

backbone 12, 24
birds 12, 20, 21, 22
breathing 14, 16, 18, 22

cartilage 19
characteristics 6
cold-blooded 14, 16, 18

eggs 14, 16, 21, 23

feathers 6, 20
fish 12, 18, 19
fur 6, 22

insects 26
invertebrates 12, 13, 24, 25, 26, 28

jellyfish 28

legs 6, 16, 26, 27

mammals 12, 22, 23

observations 6

parasites 8
phyla 13

reptiles 12, 16, 17, 18

scales 16, 18
scientists 8, 11, 24, 29
shells 16
skin 14, 16
species 8

traits 6, 28

vertebrates 12, 13, 18, 19, 20, 22, 23, 28

warm-blooded 21, 22
wings 20